this heart
belongs to:

(my heart)

Also by Ashley Rice

*girls rule ...a very special book
created especially for girls*

You Go, Girl... Keep Dreaming

Library of Congress Control Number: 2004095532
ISBN: 0-88396-845-2

Certain trademarks are used under license.

Printed in the United States of America.
First Printing: 2004

 This book is printed on recycled paper.

Blue Mountain Arts, Inc.
P.O. Box 4549, Boulder, Colorado 80306

BORDERS.

BORDERS
BOOKS MUSIC AND CAFE
5125 Jonestown Rd Suite 465
Harrisburg, PA 17112
717-541-9727

STORE: 0380   REG: 06/52   TRAN#: 6281
SALE   04/20/2009   EMP: 00016

LOVE IS ME & YOU
 9780681195868   IR T.   2.99

                Subtotal   2.99
BR: 8253428588

                Subtotal   2.99
                PA 6% TAX   .18
1 Item   Total   3.17
                CASH   10.17
                Cash Change Due 7.00

        04/20/2009 02:08PM

        Shop online
        24 hours a day
        at Borders.com

purchase price will be refunded in the form of a return gift card.

Exchanges of opened audio books, music, videos, video games, software and electronics will be permitted subject to the same time periods and receipt requirements as above and can be made for the same item only.

Periodicals, newspapers, comic books, food and drink, digital downloads, gift cards, return gift cards, items marked "non-returnable," "final sale" or the like and out-of-print, collectible or pre-owned items cannot be returned or exchanged.

Returns and exchanges to a Borders, Borders Express or Waldenbooks retail store of merchandise purchased from Borders.com may be permitted in certain circumstances. See Borders.com for details.

BORDERS.

Returns

Returns of merchandise purchased from a Borders, Borders Express or Waldenbooks retail store will be permitted only if presented in saleable condition accompanied by the original sales receipt or Borders gift receipt within the time periods specified below. Returns accompanied by the original sales receipt must be made within 30 days of purchase and the purchase price will be refunded in the same form as the original purchase. Returns accompanied by the original Borders gift receipt must be made within 60 days of purchase and the purchase price will be refunded in the form of a return gift card.

Exchanges of opened audio books, music, videos, video games, software and electronics will be permitted subject to the same time periods and receipt requirements as above and can be made for the same item only.

Periodicals, newspapers, comic books, food and drink, digital downloads, gift cards, return gift cards, items marked "non-returnable," "final sale" or the like and out-of-print, collectible or pre-owned items cannot be returned or exchanged.

Returns and exchanges to a Borders, Borders Express or Waldenbooks retail store of merchandise purchased from Borders.com may be permitted in certain circumstances.

Love Is Me and You

a very special book
for your heart from mine

Ashley Rice

Blue Mountain Press™

Boulder, Colorado

In My Heart

You don't have to be perfect to belong
in this place. You don't need to have all
the answers or always know
the right thing to say. You
can climb the highest
mountain if you want. Or
quietly imagine that you might
someday. You can take chances or
take safety nets, make miracles or
make mistakes. You don't have
to be composed at all hours to be
strong here. You don't have to be bold
or certain to be brave. You don't have to
have all the answers here or even know
who you want to be...

    just take my hand
    and rest your heart
    and stay a while with me.

When you walk into a room,
I can't take my eyes off you.
And when you turn to leave,
my affection follows you
unseen. And it's my own
truth you carry with you,
every time we part...

for it is plain to see:
you've got the key
to my heart.

Love Is Me and You

Love is
lots of things
to me.

Love is
doing things
together.

Love's like
candy.

Love is
fun,

and a challenge,
too.

Love is
sunshine

smiling on
our days,

and when
it rains

it's still
okay.

Love is lots
of things to
me, but mostly...

Love is me and you.

Maybe my heart
told your heart

it had a parking
place outside

or that we both
like taking walks

and doing things
at night.

Maybe our hearts
have the same
favorite colors

and found each
other that way.

Or maybe it was
because they both
like sunshine best

Maybe your heart
sent my heart a
secret message

Or maybe
when it comes
to things like
this

and always tell
the summer to stay.

that said: I've
been waiting for
you... let's go.

LOVE

there aren't
reasons...

hearts just know.

You Were Meant for Me

I have traveled many miles
across the shining, shining sea.
I have seen many worlds go down,
and other lives spent happily.
But the only answer that I've found
in all these places that I've seen
is that I was meant for you,
and you were meant for me.

I've followed hopes and followed hearts
and I have wandered aimlessly.
I have met strangers in strange places,
chased after even stranger dreams.

But the only certainty I've found
in all the faces that I see
is that I was meant for you,
and you were meant for me.

Now this world keeps spinning 'round.
I know the questions never cease.
But then, it all comes down to love —
from politics to poetry.
And the only answer that I've found,
the only thing I'll ever see...

is that I was meant for you,
and you were meant for me.

When It Comes to You

When it comes
to you,
there is nothing
that I wouldn't
do.

I would walk a million
miles — or a million...
and two — just to be
by your side,
just to be with you.
These things I would
do, when it comes
to you.

When it comes
to you,
there is nothing
that I wouldn't
do. Even if it took
a while, I would paint
the sky blue if it
would make you smile.
If you wanted me
to, these things I
would do.

I'd Do Almost Anything for You

For example,
I would clean
your house.

I might also
wash your car.

I'd get you
some
special
chocolates.

Or pocket you
a star.

I would
capture you a
dragonfly.

Or talk to you
all day.

I would walk
ten miles
to see you.

Or else
I'd take
the train.

I would give you
everything I have.

I'd give you
everything I've
got...

Anyway, to do all these
things... I must like you a lot.

(I do.)

Of all the fishies
in the sea...

you are my very favorite.

You are the
star of
my heart.

To You

I love the way
you look
at me...

I love the way
you smile.

I love it when
we walk along
together for
a while.

I love the
things to say
to me.

I love the
things you
do.

Mostly,
what I mean
to say
is simply:

I love you.

A Place in Your Heart

I would like to have a house with
a window to the sea and a tiny
garden right outside. I'd sit out
front and listen to the trees and
smile as the world went by. I
would like to have a place with a
window to your heart, so I would
know what you were feeling all
the time. I'd watch your days and
listen to your dreams and give you
part of everything that's mine.

I would like to have a house with
a window to the sea and a place
in your heart next to mine. By the
window, I'd give you my only key, so
you could come and visit anytime.
I would like to give you a place in
my heart, right next to the wind
and the sea. I'd sit outside on the
front porch to wait...

and smile
when I saw you coming.

complete my
heart.

Without You...

I'm peanut
butter
with no jelly.

I am one-half
of two shoes.

I'm a sock
that has
no home...
without you.

Without you,
I am salt
without
the pepper.

I am one
instead
of two.

I'm a dance
without a partner...
without you.

I am butter
with no bread.

I'm a valentine
without the red.

I am
forever blue...

without you.

If I Didn't Have You...
(The Sunflower Poem)

Without you, I would not grow so
much or laugh so much or know so
much. Without you, I would not play
so much or make so much of home.
Without you, I would not smile so
much or give so much or live so
much. So many parts of me would
be missing...

without your smile to help me grow.

You are a very special
part of my life. ☆

...When I think back on the time
before I knew you, I forget
what it was like.
...When I see you,   ♡
my eyes smile...

My heart dances...

And I know that
new chances
are born
every day.

(You're sort of like
magic, I guess.)

Thanks for being there
for me.

A poem: I love you
in the mornings...

and in   the afternoons.

I love you   in the evenings...

and when I'm working,
too.

I love you when I'm
just hanging out...

and when I've got
lots of stuff to do...

I love you
always...
every day.

Loving You

It is my
favorite thing
to do...

to spend my
time, loving
you.

I cannot
even find a
rhyme that
could do justice
to the
very thought...

...of you.

You are the
one who I
laugh with...

lean on, turn to;
...no one else
could ever
do...

I feel lucky...
loving you.

The Contents of My Heart...

In my heart, there are
hopes and thoughts and stars...
and smiles and understatements...
and all the things worth doing. In my
heart, there are dreams and smiles
and stars... and hopes and thoughts
and understatements... and all the
things worth remembering. In my
heart, there are laughs and dreams
and stars... and understanding
and understatements.
In my heart, there are
smiles and laughs and
thoughts and
stars...
and You.

That is my heart over there. It likes to be outside and to swing from trees, and sometimes, it sings in the shower. That is my heart over there. It takes walks at night and remembers things you said, and sometimes it wishes that the world were quieter. That is my heart over there. I try to hide it sometimes. I remind it that it is not invincible and it might get hurt. I tell it not to take too many chances. But it runs to love as if flowers were promises, as if it believed in high-school dances. That is my heart over there, taking your hand. Oh! It would be better to be patient, I know it! See my heart there beside your heart? It looks stronger than it is sometimes. Please be careful with it.

My heart and your heart sitting
in a tree, k-i-s-s-i-n-g...

I wish I were kissing you
right now.

If I linger a little
too long...
or I can't find the
right words to say...
if I dilly and dally
or stand my ground
acting silly when I
see you and I can't
just walk away...
if I smile and my
smile comes out all
wrong... and I no
longer know what
to do...
It's just that I
start to forget
myself every time
I look at you.

Before you came
my way...

my life was okay...

but not that grand or
anything — it wasn't
complete.

Why?

Because: you were missing.

♡

On Love
In General:

What is the exact definition
of love, I wonder?
The dictionary says that
"love," a noun, means
"deep affection" or
"fondness." It also says
"love" means "to admire,"
"delight in," and "greatly
cherish." "(My) love" is
"a person of whom one
is fond." And "to fall
in love" is "to suddenly
begin to love — to become
enamored of...."

...although all of these
things are true (I delight
in, admire, and cherish you),
I don't think love is anything
you can find in the dictionary,
really — it's just something
you know for certain
in your heart.

Looks like I'm in love...

How do I know?

When you're not
around, love can't be found...
and when I look for love,
all I see
...is you.

Love Is...

...a rocket
shooting into
outer space...

Love is
a pocket
of daisies.

Love is the
distance hearts
are willing to
go...

Love is "I'll
be there for you"...
always — not maybe.

Love is a
heart drawn
in marker on
your jeans.

Love is initials
carved into
a tree.

Love is lots of
different things. But
to me, love is
mostly...

having you.

Love is
the best part
of waking up
every day and
the best part
of going to sleep,
and the best
part of life
in general.

When I don't
feel like feeling

Or trying
at all

When life
looks too hard

And the road
seems too long

When I'm broken
in a hundred
pieces

And can't face
one more mile

You pick me
up

And put me
back together

And make
me smile

Thank You for Being There for Me

Thank you
for riding through the rough waters
of change with me.
Thank you for holding my hand.
And thank you for waiting.
Thank you
for believing in me
when I pushed you away.
Thank you for taking the time
to help me find my way.
Thank you for standing beside me.
Thank you for each day
you were there for me...

Thank you for being
there for me when
I needed you most.

Where would I be
without you?
Sad, without my best friend
to come home to.
Without your hugs,
what would I do?
Whose hand would I hold?
How could my heart
be true?
Where would I be,
without you?

Sad, without my best friend
in the world.

The **day you** came

 into my life...

the **sun** shone
brighter,

the **flowers**
opened wider,

the ⭐ stars spun
in the sky ...

and  my heart was happy.

(I'm glad to know you.)

Me and **you**:

walking through

♥ this **life** with **you**...

it is
my **favorite**
thing to do.

Always Remember

Always remember I love you,
in February, April and May;
in December and all through
the winter. In spring,
and through long summer
    days.
Always remember I love you,
and when I am far away...
know that you are
close to my heart...
        from the start,
        no one could ever
        take your place.

You
are
dear
to me

Flowers for You
(A Poem)

Flowers for the one I love...
the one I'm so often
thinking of...
the one who's in my head
as I go about my days.
A place to rest, and like
the stars above...
a light that shines for me,
in love.
(For many people I give
thanks... a hug, perhaps,
a smiling face)...
But flowers for
the one I love the
most.

I feel very lucky
to have found you...
and to spend my days
walking along with
you... and to make
my way knowing that
you are there for me,
too... and in case I
do not say it enough...

I love you.

There are many places
to go in this
world.

And there are
many things to do.

...But some of
the very best places
I've ever been...

and the very best,
most-special-days
that I've had...

...were the best
because I was
with you.

So if the world was built on love, I'd put
a little house on top... where we could sit
on the roof and watch the stars at night.
But of all those stars, sparkling in the
sky, none of them — none of them —
could ever shine as bright as you.

I believe in you.
I believe in me.
I believe some things
were meant to be.
Like the ships in the ocean,
Like the waves in the sea,
in the sea...

I believe in
you and me.

I'll never stop
loving you

no matter
what you say or do...

you have
a place in my

heart

(always ♥).

...and I want you
beside me.
and I want you
to know:
I think about you
wherever I go.
and it's your heart
I turn to.
and it's your hand
I hold.
and I love you.

I'm a little bit more
in love with you
each morning
when I wake up.

I'm a little bit more
in love with you
every time
you say my
name.

I'm a little bit more
in love with you
every time
you walk into the
room...

I'm a little bit more
    in love with you
    every day.

Because I Love You:

I love you today
  and I'll love you
  tomorrow.

I love you in good times
  and I'll love you
  in sorrow.

I will take you
  just the way you are
  or any way you choose
  to be.

Because I love you.

"For You"

Here... this is me. This is everything
I have. This is all I've got... My heart...

I give it to you.

About the Author

Ashley Rice grew up in Texas and has since lived in Northern and Southern California, New York, Massachusetts, and New Jersey, where she got her bachelor's degree in English from Princeton University.

During her college years, she created a line of greeting cards, the Ashley Rice Collection, which is published by Blue Mountain Arts and has become wildly popular. Ashley has gone on to earn a master's degree in creative writing and is the author and illustrator of the bestselling *Girls Rule*, a book of her writings and drawings that encourages girls of all ages to believe in themselves and reach for their dreams.

She currently lives in Dallas where she continues to create imaginative and original cards and books.